KU-511-767

at home

Paul Heathcote

CAPSICA

Heathcotes at home

by Paul Heathcote

Photos: Steve Dodd @ Big Cheese
Cover design: Ken Ashcroft

ISBN 0-9548431-2-6

Paul Heathcote is hereby identified as the author of this work in accordance with section 77 of the Copyright, Design and Patents Act 1988.

All rights reserved. No part of this publication may be reproduced, stored in a retrieval system or transmitted, in any form or by any means, electronic, mechanical, photocopying, recording or otherwise, without prior written permission of the publishers.

Printed and bound in Spain by Bookprint SL, Barcelona

© Paul Heathcote 2005

First published in June 2005 by Capsica Ltd
83 Ampthill Road, Liverpool L17 9QN
email: yum@capsica.net
www.capsica.net

acknowledgements

My thanks to my wife Gabbi for her patience, to Georgia and Sam for their smiles.

To Christine Thompson, my personal assistant,
for her tireless efforts and long hours.
To chefs Matt Nugent and Leigh Myers for their enormous
contribution to the photography.
To Adrian Hills for cheese advice.
To team Heathcotes for recipe testing.

http://www.heathcotes.co.uk

for news, events, recipes, full details of the restaurants and outside catering

key to quantities:

tsp = tea spoon
dsp = dessert spoon
tbsp = table spoon
ltr = litre

contents

what it's about

Simplicity sometimes just has to be the key. This is not a book aimed at stars or complicated techniques, it is a book of ingredients married together; advice and tips about how to enjoy creating a simple snack to a three course dinner. The vast majority of dishes are simple things I have picked up over the years, but some are more complicated – extracted from exciting adrenalin fuelled kitchens – that can still easily be recreated at home.

I cook far more often at home now than I do in the kitchen – after all I cannot be in them all, so it is better to be in none and influence them by taking my experiences and guiding menus, flavours, suppliers, butchers and fishmongers. It goes without saying that buying the best gives you every chance of creating something memorable, whether it is fresh herbs instead of dried, the butcher's shop well hung meat over a supermarket plastic wrapped bright red steak, or fresh fish over frozen.

Cooking at home, you don't have the advantage or the product that a restaurant has. It is a specialist profession: you can never have the time nor the manpower of a brigade of chefs, nor the expertise of a wine merchant or sommelier. So what this book does is give the home cook – and the professional in some cases – the simple ways I have collected over the last 20 years to create something special: from a soup to a sandwich, from a steak to a soufflé.

Here's an example of how the simplest of ideas can have the best results: take some really good vanilla ice cream, pour over a good measure of Pedro Ximénez sherry and serve – it's the dog's wotsits.

Hope this keeps you in the kitchen – but not for too long.

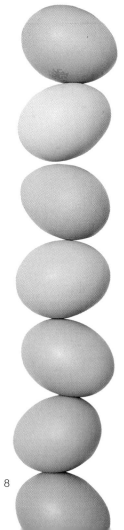

Malden sea salt Flavour is everything. The quality of your seasoning is essential. Wet the tip of your finger and dip it in ordinary table salt: the offensive taste is the additives. Repeat the exercise with pure sea salt and taste the difference.

Freshly milled pepper Pepper straight from a grinder is worlds away from ready ground. Ideally, have two mills: white pepper corns in one and black in the other. Use white on light coloured food such as fish, potatoes and cream based dishes, and black for meat, tomatoes and more robust produce.

Virgin olive oil Heating olive oil changes its flavour, so it's a waste to cook with good oil. Use cheaper olive oil or vegetable oil to cook with, and keep the expensive stuff for dressings.

Vegetable oil Vegetable oil is a neutral flavour and has a much higher heat resistance so it is great for frying and also good for light dressings. If olive oil isn't your taste, use it in the same quantities. Experiment with walnut, peanut, grapeseed oils, too.

Butter All butter in the recipes is unsalted unless stipulated. Salted butter is very obvious in desserts and butter based sauces. And do support British dairies where you can.

Milk & cream Generally I use whole milk in cooking; skimmed and semi-skimmed don't heat well and split easily. You can't whip or boil single cream, there is not enough fat in it; use whipping and double cream.

Chocolate The better the chocolate, the better the taste. Buy a good quality couveture (dark chocolate) with 70% cocoa solids.

the larder

Eggs All eggs are medium size. Use eggs at room temperature (straight from the fridge they take longer to start cooking). Buy free-range or organic, not 'farm' or 'barn' eggs.

Lemons Great for sauce making, when the sauce still lacks just a little something, a few drops of lemon juice can make all the difference. With a dash of olive oil, the best salad dressing.

Vanilla Use pods, not bottled essence. Scrape out the seeds for recipes. Keep pods, stick them in the sugar pot for wonderful flavour; and boil them for five mins in syrup for fruit salads.

Garlic Tip for peeling: cut off the root and squash the bulb a bit – lean on it with the flat of the knife. The skin almost drops off.

Herbs Keep pots on the kitchen windowsill: parsley, chives, coriander, basil. When picking, leave one or two heads on each stem to let them grow back (pick them all, it will die). Thyme, mint, rosemary, bay are hardy and are better grown outside.

Mustard French (mild), Dijon (medium), English (hot). So many brands and flavours to choose from – pick good quality. Any mustard will work to cook with – have fun experimenting.

Greek yoghurt Full fat – instead of cream or sour cream. Good to mix with mayonnaise for sharper flavour. Cook with strained cow's milk Greek yoghurt, which doesn't separate so easily.

wine

Buying and drinking wine is a fascinating and complex subject which deserves a lifetime of study, and this is only a small book.

But I am often asked for suggestions, so I have recommended wines for most of the dishes in the book. In some recipes I have mentioned a particular wine that I think marries especially well with the dish; for some I have referred to a grape variety, or perhaps the country of origin or the wine-growing region.

When it comes to price, I'd suggest that anything you buy in Britain under £3.50 is not likely to be worth drinking. Bear in mind that the bottle, the cork, label and tax will swallow £1.25 of that, before profits to grower, shipper, and retailer.

If you have £5 or £6 to spend, look for New World wines – from Chile, Australia, New Zealand or South Africa. Spend a pound or two more on Spanish or Italian, and don't bother with France until you get up to the £7-£8 mark. It's only at that point, in my opinion, that France starts to deliver decent quality.

But these are generalisations. There are always exceptions to the rule, and you can have fun exploring the dusty corners of good wine merchants and the cheaper shelves in supermarkets.

By the way – two ingredients that are really hard to match well to wine are artichokes and chocolate. I have found a couple of good wines for chocolate, but if you come across something to complement artichokes, would you please let me know.

Don't forget other options, such as beers and cider, both of which Britain can do fabulously well.

buying food

I'm a great believer in buying local. Your local butcher, greengrocer, fishmonger; the nearest farmer's market; North West producers; British, wherever possible.

Cheese, for instance. I live in the Ribble Valley, which is the centre of Lancashire cheese making, home to passionate cheese producers like Kirkhams, Butlers, Sandhams, and Bob Kitching's organic from Leagrams Dairy. British cheesemaking as a whole has been up with the world's best in the last ten years, although it's hard to beat Pont l'Eveque or a reserve Gorgonzola.

Farmers' markets have really taken a hold in the last few years, bringing new customers to local producers in town and city. Continental markets have also become popular in cities such as Liverpool, Manchester and Leeds, where you can find excellent food from Europe: French sausages to German cakes, Spanish olive oil and Italian cheeses.

Don't forget local farm shops, too. Whether they sell a few eggs or sacks of potatoes at the gate, or have a full range of fresh produce, delicatessen and drinks, they can offer great value and excellent quality.

What about organic?

In my view organic food is better as a general rule; but there are exceptions. Organic root vegetables are usually superior;

fruit can look less appealing but deliver on taste. Compare a carrot or beetroot grown in soil without pesticides and nine times out of ten it will be tastier.

A great way to buy fruit and veg is to get regular veg boxes which, as an added bonus, are usually delivered to your door. These are seasonal selections of whatever is ready that week – a lucky bag of ingredients. The choice is made for you, but the reassurance of top quality combined with the unknown is worth the fun alone. Order from local suppliers you'll find at farmers' markets; you can also find contacts in food magazines.

Organic meat, though, can be hit and miss – so much depends on the farmer and his local abattoir. Your butcher is key in buying good meat; ask for his advice.

The grower or farmer is so important in creating quality food; what I do support is the endeavours many go to. The produce is getting better year by year.

Supermarkets have improved the variety of speciality produce: it is no longer difficult to track down leaf gelatine, truffle oil, organic sugars or flours; there are dried fruits, vanilla pods, olives, cheeses in abundance.

But in my opinion, it is always important to give your support to the craftsmen and women at farmers' markets, who grow, make, cook and search for something a little bit special.

starters

soup
yellow pepper soup

olive oil
1 carrot, chopped
1 stick celery, chopped
1 onion, chopped
1kg yellow peppers,
deseeded and sliced
1 clove garlic, chopped
2 medium size potatoes
1.5 ltr chicken stock
tub of crème fraiche
chopped chives

Peel and chop the potatoes into 2cm cubes. In a large pan, with a little olive oil, put the carrot, celery, and onion. Cook on a medium light until soft, then add the peppers and garlic.

Add the potatoes and stock and cook for about 20 minutes until the potatoes are soft.

Purée in a liquidizer and (if you like your soup smooth) pass through a sieve. Season well with freshly milled pepper and sea salt as necessary.

Serve with a good spoonful of crème fraiche and chopped chives.

wine:
white Rioja

soup
clear tomato & melon juice

half a ripe galia melon
1kg over-ripe tomatoes
sprig of thyme
1 clove garlic, crushed
4 basil leaves
1 glass dry white wine

for the garnish:
galia, charentais, ogen
and watermelon
2 tomatoes
mint leaves

Put all the ingredients in a bowl, add one teaspoon of sea salt, a few turns of freshly milled pepper, and mash together well with your hands. Chill in the fridge for an hour or so.

Cover the inside of a colander or large sieve with a clean linen teatowel or square of muslin, and balance the colander over a bowl. Now tip the ingredients into the cloth and let the juices start to trickle through the cloth into the bowl.

Pull the corners of the cloth together in a knot and gently tighten it. Let it drop through in the fridge for an hour or two.

Just before serving, discard the pulp in the cloth and pour the clear juice into serving bowls.

Scoop balls from the three melons; skin and seed the two tomatoes and chop into 1cm pieces. Divide the orange, yellow and green melon balls into the bowls with the chopped tomoato and sprigs of mint.

Chef's note: Making the melon balls will give you too much for four people, but use the trimmings from the melons to double up the juice recipe; this freezes really well.

wine:
fruity dry white

soup

cream of pumpkin & sage soup

serves 4

500g pumpkin
1 small onion, chopped
half a litre of chicken stock
1 level tsp sugar
1 level tbsp corn flour
150ml cream
50g butter
olive oil
4 fresh sage leaves

sage leaves for decoration

Skin the pumpkin and cut it into large pieces; place in a hot pan with a little olive oil for about three minutes until lightly coloured.

Add the chicken stock, onion and sugar and simmer for about 15 minutes until the pumpkin and onion are cooked.

Add the cream and bring to the boil, mix the cornflour with one and a half tablespoons of water, and stir in.

Allow to cool a little before placing in a liquidiser with the butter; process for about one minute.

Return to the pan and add the finely chopped sage. Bring to the boil and season with freshly milled pepper and sea salt as necessary and finish with a drizzle of olive oil and a few sage leaves.

wine:
Italian whites
eg Soave

serves 4

fish

salad of smoked salmon
new potato and mustard cress

16 cooked new potatoes
4 slices of smoked salmon
quarter of a cucumber
1 spring onion, sliced
100g crème fraiche
1 dsp horseradish sauce
half box of mustard cress

Cut the potatoes in half and place eight pieces on to each plate.

Rip the smoked salmon pieces into half lengthways and lightly scrunch them up; put them with the potatoes.

Peel the cucumber and cut into half lengthways; remove the seeds by scraping with a teaspoon. Slice into 5mm half moons and scatter over the potatoes and salmon.

Sprinkle over the spring onions.

Make the dressing by mixing the crème fraiche and horseradish with a pinch of salt. Drizzle the dressing over the salad and sprinkle liberally with mustard cress.

wine:
New World
Chardonnay

serves 4

seared scallops with
apple & rosemary compôte

12 large scallops
mixed salad leaves (eg
curly endive, lollo rosso)

mustard dressing:
1 egg
2 tsp English mustard
100 ml peanut oil
25ml white wine vinegar

apple & rosemary compôte
see p109

For the mustard dressing, whisk the egg yolk in a bowl, add the mustard and continue whisking; slowly add the oil, whisking continuously. Whisk in the vinegar and a spoonful of warm water, and season with sea salt and freshly milled pepper.

Dress the salad leaves with a little of the mustard dressing. Place on to the centre of each plate and place three piles of apple compôte around the plate.

Season the scallops with sea salt. In a hot frying pan add a little oil and place the scallops seasoned side down and cook on that side only for about a minute until the scallops have caramelised. Turn over for a few seconds and season with a little more sea salt and lemon juice.

Place the scallops on top of the apple compôte and drizzle a little of the remaining mustard dressing around the plate. Serve immediately.

wine:
New Zealand
Sauvignon

serves 4

smoked mackerel & potato pie

350g puff pastry
350g potatoes
2 fillets smoked mackerel
2 cloves garlic
finely chopped chives
1 egg yolk
1 beaten egg
100ml double cream
4 baby gem lettuces
olive oil

Pre-heat the oven to 200°C/gas mark 6.

Roll out two circles of pastry, one slightly larger than the other. Grease a pie dish and line with the larger pastry circle.

Slice the potatoes about 3mm thick; in a large bowl mix the potatoes with the garlic, chives and season with sea salt and freshly milled pepper.

Layer the potatoes in your dish with the chunks of mackerel and cover with the pastry lid, sealing the edges. Brush the top with beaten egg; cut a cross in the middle of the lid for the steam to escape and bake for 50 minutes.

Whisk the egg yolk and cream together and put in a jug; remove the pie from the oven. Make a small funnel from greaseproof paper and hold in the steam hole; slowly pour in the cream mixture.

Return to the oven for 10 minutes, and then serve the flaky triangular wedges hot from the pan.

Dress a few baby gems with olive oil and serve.

wine:
white burgundy eg
Chablis or Mersault

Chef's note: As a vegetarian option, replace the mackerel with some more potato and lots of chopped parsley.

27

serves 4

sardines on toast

4 sardines per person
(scaled and filleted)
4 slices of granary toast
1 medium tin of tomatoes
1 clove garlic
100g feta cheese
4 leaves basil
2 leaves mint
olive oil
4 sprigs flat parsley
4 segments lemon
lemon juice
50ml balsamic vinegar

In a small pan bring the balsamic vinegar to the boil for 15-20 seconds to reduce a little, then allow to cool.

Place all the tomatoes in a sieve and squeeze all the juice from the tomatoes until really dry. Chop and place in a bowl with the crumbled feta.

Chop the garlic finely and add to the tomato along with the mint and basil, and season with sea salt and freshly milled pepper. Mix with a slug of olive oil.

Chill in the fridge for at least two or three hours.

Just before serving, fry the sardines in a little olive oil until cooked, skin side down. Season with sea salt and freshly milled pepper and a squeeze of lemon juice.

Spread a good layer of the tomato and feta mixture on the toast, place the sardines on top and decorate with a sprig of parsley and lemon segments.

To serve, decorate the plate with a drizzle of olive oil and boiled balsamic vinegar.

wine:
Portuguese white
eg Esporao

28

warm baked brie with toasted herb and almond crust

serves 2

1 individual brie (approx 125g-200g)
3 tbsp bread crumbs
2 tbsp fresh herbs
(parsley, rosemary, thyme)
1 clove garlic
1 tsp olive oil
1 tbsp flaked almonds

Toast the almonds on a metal baking tray under a hot grill until golden brown; set aside.

Meanwhile put the dried bread, herbs, almonds and garlic in a food processor and blitz to a green crumb. Slowly drizzle in the olive oil to bind the crumbs together a little.

Put the brie back in its wooden box (leaving the lid off), or in an ovenproof dish, and prick the skin with the tip of a sharp knife. Lightly season the cheese with freshly milled pepper and liberally scatter the herb crumbs over.

Place the brie in a pre heated moderate oven (180°C/gas mark 7) and bake until the crumbs are golden brown and the cheese is soft and runny in the middle.

Serve with bread sticks or crusty bread hot from the oven, or just serve with teaspoons and let your guests help themselves.

Chef's tip: This dish is ideal for sharing and can easily be served for four or six people by using several smaller cheeses or one larger cheese, your local cheese shop or delicatessen will be able to help you with this.

wine:
Alsace

31

black pudding & cheese
hash browns + caramelised pear

500g Maris Piper potatoes
1 egg white
4 slices of black pudding
100g Lancashire cheese
2 tsp chopped chives
2 tsp chopped parsley
1 ripe conference pear
2 tsp icing sugar

simple butter sauce:
see p112

Leave the potatoes in their skins and cook in boiling water for 10 minutes so that they are still firm. Drain and peel. Grate the potatoes into a bowl and mix with half the herbs.

Add a pinch of sea salt to the egg white, beat with a whisk and mix with the grated potato; season with sea salt and freshly milled pepper.

Pat out a quarter of the mix in a circle larger than the black pudding. Place pudding and 25g of cheese in the middle, fold over the potatoes and pat into a circle.

Deep fry at 160°C until golden brown.

Scoop the pear into balls; put one dessertspoon of vegetable oil into a hot frying pan with one spoon of sieved icing sugar. When the sugar turns golden brown, add the pear balls and toss quickly until caramelised.

Mix the remaining herbs into the butter sauce.

Serve the hash browns with a few caramelised balls of pear, the herby butter sauce, and large sprigs of flat leaf parsley.

wine:
Alsace, Riesling or
Gewürztraminer

32

chicken
torn chicken salad with blue cheese & gems

1 small roasted chicken
2 baby gem lettuces
2 slices white bread
4 slices smoked streaky
bacon cut into 1cm strips
100g soft blue cheese (eg
Gorgonzola)
4 dsp Greek yoghurt
olive oil
1 clove garlic, crushed

Cut the sliced bread into 1cm cubes and shallow fry with the bacon in a little olive oil until golden brown. Drain on to kitchen paper.

Cut the bottom off the gems, wash, pat dry, separate the leaves and toss in a bowl with a little olive oil.

Divide the leaves between six plates and using your fingers tear the chicken breast into strips and scatter these, with the bacon and croutons, over the gems.

Beat the blue cheese in a bowl until smooth then fold in the yoghurt and garlic. Add a dash of water to take the dressing to pouring consistency. Drizzle over the salad and season with a pinch of sea salt and freshly milled black pepper.

wine:
fruity whites eg
Viognier

ham

potted ham with tarragon & soft green peppercorns

1 small knuckle of ham
1 onion
3 cloves
1 pack unsalted butter
2 tsp English mustard
12 soft green peppercorns
2 good pinches nutmeg
1 tsp chopped tarragon

Cook the ham: place the knuckle in a large pan, fill with cold water and bring to the boil for 2-3 minutes. Remove from the heat and drain (this helps remove some of the salt). Fill the pan again with cold water, add the onion and cloves and bring to the boil; simmer for about 90 minutes, or until cooked.

Meanwhile on a low heat melt the butter in a pan, then allow to stand for 10 minutes; the butter will separate and a milky residue will sink to the bottom, leaving clarified butter on top. Ladle the clarified butter into a jug, leaving behind most of the milky solids.

When the ham is cooked, drain it, scrape off most of the fat and put about 300g in a food processor with all the other ingredients. Pulse the mixture for about 10 seconds, add half of the butter, scrape the sides and pulse again for a few more seconds until the ham is thoroughly chopped. Check seasoning and add sea salt if necessary and freshly milled pepper.

Scrape into a pot or individual ramekins, top with the rest of the melted butter and chill overnight.

Serve with toast or warm crusty bread.

wine:
chilled Beaujolais

36

mains

pan fried salmon
with mushroom sauce

serves 4

approx 200g of salmon per person

mushroom sauce:
see p115

Remove all the scales from the salmon using the back of a spoon or blunt knife. Remove any bones from the fillets using a pair of tweezers or pliers.

To cook, put in a hot pan skin side down, with a little oil, until golden and crisp – approximately five minutes.

Flip over for a further 30 seconds and add a squeeze of lemon juice and re-season with sea salt.

Serve on a bed of warm mushroom sauce, and top with a sprig of flat leaf parsley or dill.

wine:
Chassagne Montrachet,
Chardonnay,
or Chablis

40

fish

skate wings with lemon pickle

*1 large skate wing filleted
into two pieces
25g butter
olive oil
chopped parsley*

*lemon pickle:
see p108*

Take a hot frying pan, add a little oil, season the skate with salt
and pepper and cook on one side until crispy and golden
brown.

Turn over and cook for a further minute and remove from
the pan.

Wipe the pan clean and add the butter, sizzle until starting to
brown; add four dessertspoons of lemon pickle and when hot,
spoon over the skate and finish with chopped parsley.

*wine:
crisp whites, eg
Sauvignon*

serves 4

goat's cheese & leek risotto

100g unsalted butter
1 clove garlic
2 shallots
1 large leek sliced in rings
250g arborio rice
half glass white wine
250ml vegetable stock
100ml warm goat's milk
glug of olive oil
bunch chopped chives
100g goat's cheese

Chop the shallots and garlic finely and sweat them with the leek in butter until soft, but make sure they don't colour.

Add rice and cook for about one minute, until it has turned transparent. Add white wine and stir in until it has all been soaked up.

Add stock a little at a time, stirring constantly until all is absorbed then repeat with the milk until the rice is cooked and creamy. Add more stock than the recipe if the rice is still slightly undercooked. Season with sea salt and freshly milled pepper and a little olive oil.

Stir in the crumbled goat's cheese 20-30 seconds before serving. Sprinkle with chopped chives.

Chef's note: Goat's cheese can vary in strength from very mild to strong, and can be soft or hard, so experiment with different cheeses each time you make this. Personally, I like to use the mild crumbly cheese of Delamere for this dish.

wine:
Frascati, Viognier

pasta
spaghetti piedmontese

50g butter
half an onion
2 cloves garlic
250g spinach
8 sage leaves
pinch of nutmeg
parmesan cheese
500g spaghetti

In a heavy pan melt half of the butter, add the finely chopped onions and crushed garlic and sizzle for about one minute.

Remove the stalks from the spinach; add the leaves to the onions and stir well before adding the sage.

Season with nutmeg and a little salt and pepper.

Cook for one or two minutes until the spinach is wilted; remove from the heat. Drain well to remove any water; place in a food processor and puree.

Meanwhile cook the spaghetti in plenty of boiling salted water until cooked but still firm (al dente), drain, stir in the remaining butter and check the seasoning.

Stir in the spinach and serve immediately with plenty of grated parmesan.

wine:
Prosecco

chicken

one hour herb roasted chicken

serves 4

olive oil
1 carrot
1 chicken 1.5-2kg (3.5 lb)
25g butter
25g soft cream cheese
good sprig tarragon
good sprig chervil
good sprig rosemary
zest of half a lemon

buttered peas:
see p80

wine:
full fruity white eg
48   Chilean Chardonnay

Switch the oven to 180°C/gas mark 5 and place roasting tray in oven to heat up.

Chop the herbs finely and mix with the cream cheese, butter and finely grated zest; season well with salt and pepper.

To prepare the chicken remove the parson's nose and trim up any excess fat. Loosen the skin from the breast by gently working your fingers over the meat and under the skin to make a pocket; repeat on the other side. Stuff the herb mix evenly under both breasts.

With a sharp knife, score the legs with two or three incisions: this will make the legs crispy and allow them to cook quicker. Tie up the legs. Rub olive oil over the chicken and season with salt and pepper.

Place the chicken on its side on the hot roasting tray with the thigh of the chicken pressed firmly down. Use the carrot to balance the chicken and stop the breast falling on to the tray.

Cook for 25 minutes before turning over: repeat for around 20 minutes. Sit the chicken upright for a further 15 minutes. Check that the bird is cooked by inserting a small knife into the wing knuckle of the bird to test for blood.

Allow to rest at room temperature for 10 minutes or so.

Carve into four portions and serve with buttered peas.

serves 2

Goosnargh corn-fed chicken
with wild mushrooms & leeks

*2 breasts of Goosnargh
chicken
75g butter
1 tbsp shallot
dash of white wine
50ml water
25ml whipping cream
50g wild mushrooms
4 cooked baby leeks
2 tsp fresh tarragon
squeeze of lemon juice*

In a heavy pan melt 25g of the butter and seal the chicken breast, skin side down.

Add finely chopped shallots and white wine.

Bring to the boil, add water, cover with a lid and place in the oven at 180°C until cooked (10-15 minutes).

Remove chicken and strain liquid through a sieve into another pan. Bring to the boil and add the mushrooms and cook for about one minute before adding the cream and boiling.

Whisk in the butter little by little, add the cooked leeks, chicken and finely shredded tarragon. Season with sea salt and freshly milled pepper, and a few drops of lemon juice.

*wine:
white Burgundy eg
Meursault*

duck

roast breast of duckling with dumplings, roots & apple sauce

2 double crowns of duck breast per person

dumplings (makes 30):
150ml water
1 shallot finely diced
80g butter
150g flour
4 eggs
50g cooked ham or duck
2 tsp chopped parsley

duckling

Cook the duck breast in a pan or roasting dish skin side down and roast at 225°C/gas mark 7-8 for about 10-15 minutes; let it cool.

To remove the breasts from the bone, insert a small knife along the backbone; using the tip of the knife, slowly ease the meat away. Trim any sinew from underneath the breast bone.

Place on a grill tray fat upwards ready to be grilled to a crisp finish, just before serving.

dumplings

Bring the water, finely chopped shallots and butter to the boil until the butter has melted. Add flour, beat in well and remove from the heat. Allow to cool a little by placing in a bowl. Beat the eggs in well one by one. Season with salt and pepper, add the chopped ham and parsley. Place the mix in a piping bag with a plain 2cm nozzle.

Bring a large pan of water to the boil and using a small knife

wine:
Tokaj,
Pinot Gris,
Beaujolais

in one hand pipe 3cm long dumplings into the water, using the tip of the knife to help shape them.

Cook in the water for about two minutes before lifting out and draining onto kitchen paper.

Pat dry and then fry lightly in olive oil before serving.

apple juice sauce

Dissolve the arrowroot in a little cold water. Boil the apple juice and stock until it has reduced by half. Add the arrowroot; whisk in the butter, and serve.

onions and turnips

Peel and boil the onions and turnips. Keep the turnips hot in a little hot water and a knob of butter, with a lid on the pan. Caramelise the onions by putting them in a hot frying pan with a spoonful of vegetable oil and a teaspoon of caster sugar. Season and toss until golden.

to serve

Put a spoonful of apple & rosemary compôte in the centre of the plate. Cut the duckling in half and pile it on top. Scatter the dumplings, onions and turnips, and pour over the juice.

See overleaf for illustration

apple juice sauce:
150ml apple juice
150ml chicken stock
half tsp of arrowroot
2 tsp butter

18 baby onions
18 baby turnips

apple & rosemary compôte
see p109

Chef's note: This is more of a challenge than most of the recipes in the book, but it is a splendid and very impressive dinner party dish; well worth the effort.

roast breast of duckling with dumplings, baby onions and turnips in an apple juice sauce

ham shanks in cider with cloves

2 ham shanks
400ml cider
1 onion
2 bay leaves
1 dsp muscovado sugar
about 8 peppercorns
12 cloves

mustard butter:
see p110

The day before: remove the outside skin from the ham shanks leaving the majority of fat in place; cover in cold water in a large pan and soak overnight to help remove some of the salt.

On the day: discard the water, wash the shanks and return to the pan. Pour over the cider and top up with cold water so the meat is just covered.

Add the onion, bay leaves, sugar and peppercorns, bring to the boil and simmer for about two hours until cooked; every so often top up with a little water to keep the meat covered.

When cooked, remove the shanks and continue to boil the liquid. Reduce till there's only about a mug full left in the pan.

With the point of sharp knife, criss-cross the fat of the ham, push in the cloves and brush with the cider liquid.

Roast in a hot oven at 200°C/gas mark 7 for 20 minutes or until golden brown, basting with any remaining cider from time to time.

Serve with boiled potatoes and mustard butter.

wine:
cider or
sweet German wine

pork
sticky garlic ribs

1kg ribs of pork
5 cloves garlic
1 red chilli
5cm fresh ginger root
100ml dry sherry
3 dsp honey
200ml hoisin sauce
200g muscovado sugar
1 tsp Chinese five spice
50ml sesame oil

Place the ribs in a pan of water, bring to boil and cook for about 40 minutes. Skim off any scum that appears.

Meanwhile gently cook the finely chopped garlic, ginger and chilli with the sesame oil for one or two minutes.

Remove from the heat and add the remaining ingredients.

Drain the ribs and whilst warm toss in the marinade and leave to chill overnight.

On the day: roast in an oven about 180°C/gas mark 5 for 20 minutes until slightly charred and sticky.

Chef's note: These are so delicious that you might find you need to make twice the amount.

59

pork

honey & herb roasted pork with crackling

2.5kg loin end of pork
(about 5lb) with crackling
olive oil
2 dsp honey
handful organic brown
sugar
2 glasses white wine
200ml water
small bunch fresh herbs
(parsley, rosemary, thyme)
1 dsp corn flour

Pre heat the oven to 220°C/gas mark 7.

To make perfect crackling remove the skin from the loin by cutting away in one piece. Score well with the point of a sharp knife and place on a wire rack over a roasting tray. Brush with a little oil and sprinkle with sea salt. Roast until crisp and golden and put to one side.

Meanwhile roast the pork: place fat side upwards in a roasting tray and again using the tip of a sharp knife criss-cross the fat about 5mm deep. Season with sea salt and freshly milled pepper and roast for about one hour until almost cooked.

Remove from the oven and spoon the honey over the fat and sprinkle on the sugar. Add the wine and water to the roasting tray and cook for a further 15 minutes until golden.

Press the herbs on to the pork and return to the oven for another 10 minutes. Lift the pork out of the tray and keep warm.

Dissolve the corn flour with a tablespoon of water and whisk into the roasting tray liquid, scraping off any of those juicy caramelised bits that have stuck; pass through a sieve and into a pan. Boil, and skim the fat from the top.

Carve the pork and serve with juices and crackling.

wine:
Chardonnay
Sauvignon Blanc or
light reds eg
Pinot Noir

lamb
best end of lamb
in provençale herb crumbs

1 loin or best end of lamb,
on the bone, fat removed
1 egg white
1 clove garlic
sprig thyme
sprig rosemary
approx 30g parsley
2 slices dried white bread
good glug of olive oil

Place all the ingredients into a food processor except the olive oil. Chop to a fine green crumb then slowly add the olive oil.

Season the lamb with sea salt and freshly milled pepper. Lightly whisk the egg white; dip the lamb into the egg white and roll in the herb crumbs, pressing firmly.

Gently roast on a lightly greased tray about 150-160°C/gas mark 3-4 for 10 minutes until pink.

wine:
full bodied red eg
Rioja, Rhone, or
Bordeaux

lamb

Irish stew with onion dumplings

serves 4

4 pieces neck lamb
4 lamb cutlets
2 onions cut into quarters
2 small carrots
2 sticks celery
1 leek
2 small potatoes
750g chicken stock
20g pearl barley
small sprig rosemary
flat leaf parsley
half medium onion
120g self raising flour
60g beef or vegetable suet
small bunch parsley
half tsp English mustard
approx 80ml water

Season the meat; coat in a little flour and fry off in oil until light brown.

Wash and trim the vegetables into equal size; cube the potatoes into 2.5 cm chunks.

Place the neck in a casserole dish. Add the vegetables on top, season with sea salt and freshly milled pepper, place the cutlets on top of the vegetables. Pour in the stock and sprinkle in the barley.

Cook on a low light for about two hours, until the lamb is very tender and the barley is very soft.

Meanwhile boil the onion for about one minute, in just enough water to cover; drain well.

Mix the flour and suet together, add the parsley and mustard and bind together with the water.

Season with sea salt and freshly milled pepper and roll into a round about 3-4cm long.

Cut into 2cm thick rounds when ready to bake.

To finish push the dumplings on to the top of the stew and bake for about 15-20 minutes until crusty.

wine:
Guinness
or wheat beer

64

lamb
leg of lamb steaks with lemon & garlic

serves 2

2 x 200g leg lamb steaks
1 clove garlic
zest of 1 lemon
juice of half a lemon
2 dsp olive oil
sprig fresh rosemary

cous cous:
see p76

yoghurt dressing:
see p107

With the point of a sharp knife make a few incisions across each lamb steak.

Pour over the lemon juice, zest, crushed garlic, finely chopped rosemary and olive oil. Season with a little sea salt and freshly milled pepper and leave to marinate for 15 minutes.

Heat a griddle pan or frying pan with a little oil, cook the lamb on the opposite side of the incisions and griddle well. Flip over and cook the remaining side which has the garlic and lemon for 30 seconds to a minute.

Serve with cous cous and yoghurt dressing.

wine:
light red from Italy
or Spain

the secret to the perfect steak

As a rough guide to cooking times, for a 25mm (one inch) thick steak, on a smoking hot griddle or frying pan:

Blue:
90 seconds
flip over for 30 seconds

Rare:
2.5 minutes
flip over for 30 seconds

Medium rare:
3.5 minutes
flip over for 30 seconds

Medium/well done:
4.5 minutes
flip over for 30-60 seconds

Cooking a delicious steak isn't really that difficult if you stick to a couple of golden rules. Good quality meat, a smoking hot pan, and cooking mainly on one side.

For the perfectly cooked steak, indulge in really good quality beef. I'd suggest one of the following cuts: rib eye, fillet or sirloin. Make sure you use a good butcher: good meat, properly hung, will give you the quality, whatever breed it comes from.

How long you need to cook the steak will depend a bit on the cut, but mostly on how thick the steak is, and how rare or well done your guests or family like it.

Heat your griddle or frying pan till it's smoking hot before cooking the meat. It must be the highest possible temperature (without setting the pan on fire...) to cook well.

Too many steaks in a pan will drop the temperature and they will quite literally stew in their own juices rather than frying.

Cook your steak on one side and flip it over only for the last few seconds.

Don't add oil to the pan. On one side only, brush the steak lightly with oil and season with sea salt and freshly milled pepper – and put the steak in the pan seasoned side down.

Don't fiddle with it in the pan – leave it alone till you have to flip it over.

For a well-done steak (charred but still juicy) flip it over when a couple of millimetres at the top of the steak is still raw – not before – otherwise it will dry out.

Always try to cook your steak a little less than you want it, then allow it to rest for a couple of minutes. This will help retain the juices, and allow the meat to relax, making it more tender. It is still hot, and will continue to cook inside a little, so that it will be the perfect finish when served.

The perfect steak, well seasoned, is delicious as it is, but try it also with marmite (see photo above), herb or mustard butter, au poivre, or with a madeira sauce.

Serve with a green salad or lightly cooked green beans, spinach or spring cabbage.

beef

steak au poivre

2 rump sirloin/fillet steaks
25g butter
1 shallot
8 black peppercorns
8 white peppercorns
dash of brandy
half glass red wine
100ml double cream
soft green peppercorns

wine:
without question, the
best wine for this is
from the Douro in
Portugal – Quinta do
Crasto Touriga
Nacional (a very
special treat), or the
more affordable
Reserva.
Otherwise: a peppery
red Rhone

Crush the white and black peppercorns. Press the peppercorns and a little sea salt into the steaks and cook in a hot frying pan (see p68) until rare.

Remove the steaks from the pan and place to one side.

Turn down the heat; add the butter and finely chopped shallots and fry for about 15-20 seconds, until the shallots are soft but not coloured.

Add the brandy, then the red wine; boil until the liquid reduces by half before adding the cream.

If the steaks need more cooking for your liking, place them back in the pan with the juices and cook further (see timing guidelines on p68).

Season the sauce with sea salt, add the green peppercorns.

Chef's tip: If you have no pestle and mortar, use a heavy rolling pin. Or place the peppercorns on a flat surface and rock a heavy bottomed pan over the top to crush well.

sides
gratin dauphinoise

400g potatoes (Maris
Piper or Desiree)
1 clove garlic
200ml milk
200ml whipping cream

Peel and slice the potatoes about 3mm thick.

In a heavy bottomed pan bring the cream, milk and crushed garlic to the boil and add a good pinch of sea salt and freshly milled pepper.

Add the potatoes and bring back to the boil, making sure they don't stick to the bottom. Re-check the seasoning (NB don't overseason: the cream will concentrate the flavour and make it more salty).

Place in a casserole dish and bake at 180°C/gas mark 5-6 for about 30-40 minutes or until cooked. The potatoes are done when you insert a small knife and it slides in and out easily.

sides
grilled polenta cake

50g onion
2 cloves garlic chopped
10g butter
250g instant polenta
half litre boiling water
50g grated parmesan
small bunch basil
50g pine kernels
olive oil

Gently toast the pine kernels under a hot grill until golden brown. Chop the garlic and onions finely, and gently cook them with the butter until soft but colourless.

Add the polenta, then slowly add the boiling water until a firm paste is formed. Add the parmesan, the finely shredded basil, pine nuts and seasoning with salt and pepper.

Place on a tray and spread out about 2cm thick and allow to cool. When set, cut into portions and grill with a little olive oil and serve.

favourite cous cous

serves 4

25g butter
half an onion
2 cloves garlic
50g cooked peas
50g cooked broad beans
25g cooked sweetcorn
25g whole almonds
25g raisins
6 green olives quartered
4 leaves mint
125g cous cous

yoghurt dressing:
see p107

Check the maker's recipe for cous cous and measure out the water for 125g cous cous (recommendations vary slightly, but it is normally about equal quantities).

In a thick-bottomed pan, gently fry the chopped onions and garlic in the butter for one minute.

Add the peas, beans, corn, raisins, nuts and olives followed by the water, bring to the boil and remove from the heat. Add the mint and cous cous and give a good stir before placing a lid on top and leave for three minutes.

The cous cous will now be cooked. Season with sea salt and freshly milled pepper and serve with lamb (see p64) and Greek yoghurt dressing.

Chef's note: This cous cous is also great with grilled steak, chicken and fish, or as a side dish with a barbecue.

sides

carrots with tarragon & garlic

8 medium carrots
1 clove garlic
1 sprig tarragon
pinch of sugar
25g butter

Peel the carrots but leave them whole.

Place all the ingredients in a pan with half a teaspoon of sea salt, cover with just enough water and cook until just firm – continuing to add enough water to keep the carrots covered.

When almost cooked remove carrots from the water, boil the liquid and reduce by two thirds, then place the carrots back in the liquid to glaze and re-heat.

sides
four green veg

all recipes serve 4

buttered peas with lettuce:
1 tsp white wine vinegar
2 tsps white wine
1 bay leaf
1 shallot
half tsp English mustard
half an iceberg lettuce
2 tsp double cream
100g hard unsalted butter
250g cooked peas

spinach with garlic:
200g spinach
1 clove garlic

cabbage with bacon:
1 Savoy cabbage
2 rashers streaky bacon
20g butter

fine beans with shallots:
150g fine (French) beans
1 shallot
20g butter

buttered peas with lettuce

Place the vinegar, wine, finely chopped shallot and bay leaf in a small pan and boil until only a teaspoon of the liquid remains; add the mustard. Add the finely shredded lettuce and cream and bring back to the boil for 15 seconds. Whisk in the diced butter gradually. Season; reheat the peas and add to the sauce.

spinach with garlic

Spear a clove of garlic on the end of a fork. Wash the spinach well and put in a pan with the butter. Stir with the fork, season with salt and pepper, and cook for one or two minutes till wilted.

savoy cabbage with bacon

Cut bacon into 1cm strips and fry till crisp in a little oil. Shred the cabbage; put in a pan with the butter and a dash of water. Cover with lid, occasionally adding another dash of water, for three minutes. Add bacon and onions; season. Boil till water has evaporated and only the butter remains.

fine green beans with shallots

Chop the shallots finely and fry till soft but still colourless. Steam or boil the beans and top with the shallots before serving.

sides

braised beetroot with sour cream

6 medium beetroot,
topped and tailed and
peeled with a knife
25g butter
half glass of red wine
half onion
2 cloves garlic
dsp balsamic vinegar
1 tsp demerara sugar
sprig thyme
4 black peppercorns
sour cream

Top and tail and peel the beetroot, slice the garlic finely, chop the onions and crush the black peppercorns.

Place the peeled beetroot in a large pocket of aluminium foil along with all the other ingredients.

Seal tightly and place in an ovenproof dish with a generous amount of water to prevent burning the foil.

Bake at 160-170°C/gas mark 6 for about 1.5 hours. Then open the foil with caution as the steam could burn. Test with a sharp knife to see if the beetroot is cooked and soft, otherwise return to the oven until cooked.

At the last moment spoon over a good spoonful of sour cream or crème fraiche with a little of the roasting liquid.

Chef's tip
To prevent red colouring on your hands, a pair of rubber gloves or thin latex gloves are great for peeling beetroot.

afters

classics
trifle

20 trifle sponges
3 punnets fresh raspberries
squeeze of lemon juice
60g sugar
200ml sweet sherry

400ml double cream
100ml milk
1 vanilla pod
6 yolks
50g sugar
2 heaped dsp corn flour
dash of water

to decorate:
whipped double cream
sprigs of mint
grated chocolate

First make the raspberry coulis. Put one punnet of raspberries in a very hot, dry pan. Add lemon juice and sugar and cook rapidly for one minute. Whisk, then pass through a sieve and chill.

Mash the sponges with one punnet of fresh raspberries and the sweet sherry.

Place a spoonful of coulis in the bottom of a glass tumbler for each person, along with three raspberries. Divide the sponge mix between each dish and spoon in any remaining coulis plus another raspberry, and chill.

Make the custard by bringing the cream, milk and seeds from vanilla pod to the boil. Whisk together the egg yolks and sugar. Moisten the corn flour with a dash of water and add to the yolks. Pour a dash of the boiled cream to the yolks and whisk well before returning all to the pan and cooking until thick. Allow to cool before dividing the mix between the dish; refrigerate until ready to serve.

Top with whipped double cream, raspberries, mint and scatter grated chocolate.

Chef's tip: out of season you can use 225g frozen raspberries instead of fresh ones, or any soft fruit eg strawberries or blackcurrants (but you may need a tiny bit more sugar).

wine:
Muscat or Barsac

classics
favourite bread & butter pudding

5 thin slices white bread
75g butter
100g sultanas
3 eggs
220ml milk
220ml cream
50g caster sugar
1 vanilla pod
25g icing sugar
50g apricot jam

chocolate version:
as above, plus
100g grated chocolate
muscovado, not caster
1 level tsp mixed spice
50g cocoa powder

wine:
Sauternes or Barsac
with the classic
Bagnols with the
chocolate version

Split the vanilla pod and scrape out the seeds. Butter the bread and remove the crusts. Place one layer of bread on the base of the tray and cover with a layer of sultanas. Place the rest of the bread on top of the sultanas.

Bring the cream, milk, sugar and vanilla seeds to the boil in a pan and place the eggs in a bowl and whisk the hot liquid into them. Pour the egg mixture over the bread and place the dish in a bain-marie (or a roasting dish half full of water) and put in a moderate oven for about half an hour until cooked.

Dust with icing sugar and glaze until golden. Spread thickly with apricot jam.

Serve with clotted cream and a compôte of dried apricots.

Chef's note: For a change, try the spicy chocolate version: The method is almost identical, but replace 50g of the sultanas with 100g of grated dark chocolate on the bottom layer of bread. Use dark muscovado sugar instead of white caster sugar; and add the mixed spice and cocoa powder in with the cream, milk, sugar and vanilla when you make the custard (see photo inset).

Serve with whipped cream and Armagnac prunes (see p117).

chocolate
simple chocolate pots

100g dark chocolate
250ml double cream
40g muscovado sugar
1 vanilla pod
1 egg
fresh raspberries
icing sugar
mint

Place the chocolate in the food processor and chop into small pieces.

Meanwhile place the cream, sugar and vanilla seeds into a pan and bring to the boil.

Pour into the food processor and leave for one minute. Switch on and add the egg for a further 20 seconds.

Pour into small ramekins and chill for at least two hours, or preferably overnight.

Dust with icing sugar and decorate with raspberries and mint.

Chef's tip: for deliciously bitter chocolate pots, omit the extra muscovado sugar.

chocolate
chocolate crunch torte
with pistachios & sour cherries

225g dark chocolate
10g unsalted pistachios
50g dried sour cherries
50g raisins
3 tablespoons rum
50g butter
150ml double cream
225g sweet oat biscuits

You'll need a loose based cake tin (20cm in diameter, 4cm deep) lightly greased with a flavourless oil.

Soak the dried cherries and raisins in the rum overnight.

Place the broken-up chocolate and butter in a large heat proof bowl over a saucepan of barely simmering water, making sure the bowl doesn't touch the water. Allow the chocolate to melt – it should take about five minutes.

Remove from the heat, give the chocolate a good stir and let it cool for a couple of minutes. Fold in the lightly whipped cream followed by the soaked fruits, chopped pistachios and broken biscuits, and mix well.

Spoon the mixture into the cake tin evenly, cover with cling film and chill for a minimum of four hours.

Serve with a good spoonful of crème fraiche.

wine:
Quady Black
Muscat

rhubarb & strawberry mille-feuille

serves 4

400ml water
200g caster sugar
few drops rosewater
2 sticks rhubarb
strawberry coulis
100g strawberries
25g unsalted pistachios
4 filo sheets per person
icing sugar
25g toasted flaked almonds
25g melted butter

honey & vanilla yoghurt and strawberry coulis:
see p116

Cut the rhubarb into 10cm (exactly) pieces. Bring the water, sugar and rosewater to the boil and add the rhubarb sticks. Leave on the heat for a further 30 seconds before removing and allow to cool. When cold, chill on kitchen cloth, and put the syrup to one side.

You need two filo leaves per person. For the top tier of the mille-feuille leaves, take a sheet of filo pastry; brush with melted butter, place another sheet on top, brush again with melted butter and add a slight sprinkling of icing sugar. Sprinkle over a few flaked almonds and chill until the butter has set – about 2-3 minutes.

Cut into 10cm x 5cm rectangles and bake until light brown.

For the base of the mille-feuille repeat, but omit the icing sugar and almonds.

To assemble the mille-feuille:

Place two dessertspoons of honey and vanilla yoghurt on the base filo leaf, followed by two pieces of rhubarb and two wild strawberries. Top with the almond filo leaf.

Decorate with a drizzle of rosewater syrup, a drizzle of strawberry coulis, a few wild strawberries, pistachios or toasted and sugared whole almonds.

wine:
Quady Orange Muscat

fruit

apple jelly with cinnamon cream

300ml sweet apple juice
15g gelatine
50g caster sugar
rind and juice of 1 lemon
3 egg whites
seeds of 1 vanilla pod
250ml whipping cream
25g caster sugar
half tsp ground cinnamon

Put the apple juice and the gelatine in a small saucepan and leave to soak for five minutes. Add the sugar, lemon rind and juice. Place the pan over a low heat and allow the gelatine and sugar to dissolve, but don't allow the mixture to boil.

Remove from the heat and strain into a large mixing bowl; then leave until cold.

Add the egg whites and with an electric mixer whisk the jelly until it is very foamy and beginning to set. (This will take at least 10 minutes but you can speed things up by putting the bowl over a second bowl of ice.)

Pour into individual glass dishes and chill for 3-4 hours before serving.

Split the vanilla pod and with a small knife scrape out the seeds. In a large bowl whisk the cream, vanilla seeds and sugar until just soft and ribbon like, add the cinnamon and stir in.

Serve with the apple jelly.

wine:
late harvest Muscat

fruit
hot banana soufflé

100ml water
1 dessertsp cornflour
2 small ripe bananas
6 egg whites
25g + 150g caster sugar
25g unsalted butter
lemon juice

Soften the butter and grease the ramekins; put a spoonful of caster sugar into each ramekin and roll around until it is evenly lined. Tip the remainder into another and repeat until all four are well lined using more sugar if necessary.

Mixing the water and cornflour; put into a food processor with the ripe bananas and a squeeze of lemon juice. Blitz to a smooth pulp, scraping down once or twice if required.

Scald a clean mixing bowl with boiling water and dry it, to make sure it isn't greasy. Put the egg whites in the bowl and start to whisk. Gradually add the 150g sugar and a squeeze of lemon juice until you have a smooth soft peak meringue.

In another large bowl measure out four heaped dessertspoons of banana pulp, take a third of the meringue and mix thoroughly to achieve a paste.

Gently fold in the remaining meringue and divide between the ramekins. Smooth off the top to create a flat surface and run your thumb around the edge of the soufflés to make sure the edge does not stick to the sides (this will also help the soufflés rise straight).

Keep the soufflés in a fridge until needed. When ready to bake, space them out on a tray and bake at 180°C-200°C for 10-15 minutes, until risen. Serve immediately.

wine:
Jurançon

fruit
lemon & lime posset

560ml double cream
150g caster sugar
zest and juice of 1 lemon
zest and juice of 2 limes

In a pan, bring the cream and sugar to the boil and simmer for two minutes.

Remove from the heat and stir in all the juice and zest.

Allow to cool before pouring into small ramekins or wine glasses and chill for 4-5 hours or overnight.

Serve with shortbread biscuits.

Chef's tip: Experiment by adding different fruits at the bottom of the glass – bananas, peaches, strawberries and blueberries would all be delicious.

wine:
Riesling Eiswein

cheese
British cheese board

F Fresh cheeses – made mainly from goat's milk they are eaten days after making. Soft and mousse-like in texture.

WH Soft white rind cheeses – Brie style cheese, rind on the outside and soft in the middle, ripened over weeks.

W Wash rind cheeses – matured over weeks, can be semi soft or firm bodied. Dipped or smeared with wash to impart flavour or aroma; each dip is the speciality of the maker. Whisky, cider, wine and pear juice are well known examples.

H Classical hard cheeses – two groups, hard pressed and crumbly: the core of traditional British cheese making. Hard: matured around four months to two years; often cloth bound, or waxed. Crumbly: matured over six to ten weeks and waxed.

B Blue cheeses – two styles: firm bodied (Stilton) or semi soft (Garstang Blue). The blue mould is sprayed onto the curd during cheese making and each cheese sealed after production. The mould only grows once the cheese has been pierced with needles to allow oxygen in, therefore creating perfect conditions for the moulds to grow.

wine: heavy reds eg bordeaux or cabernet sauvignon; port and sauternes work well too, especially with blue veined cheeses

extras

biscuits

parmesan & cheddar biscuits

50g grated red cheddar
50g grated Parmesan
50g plain flour
50g unsalted butter
flour for rolling
pinch of cayenne pepper

Put all the ingredients in a bowl and rub together well. Mould into a ball of cling film and rest for 30 minutes in a fridge.

Roll out the dough about 3-4mm thick and cut out biscuits with a 6cm cutter. Put them on to a lightly greased tray, prick each one once with a fork and bake for about 10 minutes or until light brown at 180°C.

Lift onto a cooking wire to cool before serving.

dressings

Greek yoghurt dressing

Peel and grate the cucumber, season with some salt and leave in a mixing bowl for about 10 minutes to draw out some of the water.

Squeeze out the excess water from the cucumber and leave to one side. Crush the garlic with a little sea salt and finely chop the mint leaves.

Mix all the above with the yoghurt and add the grated lemon zest. Season with sea salt and freshly milled pepper if desired.

60g Greek yoghurt
half cucumber
zest of half a lemon
few sprigs of mint
1 clove garlic

coriander & chilli dip

Put water, chilli, garlic, creamed coconut and ginger into a food processor and blitz well, scraping down and repeating. Add the herbs, juice and zest; blitz again. Season with a pinch of sea salt and blitz for another 30 seconds.

Serve with grilled meats and fish, or with hot new potatoes on forks.

NB This keeps well in the fridge, but it may need 10 seconds in the microwave before serving.

2 tbsp hot water
1 green chilli deseeded
4 cloves garlic
2cm ginger root
80g creamed coconut
handful fresh coriander
10 mint leaves
zest of 1 lime
juice of 3 limes

lemon pickle

8 lemons
2 dsp salt
1 tsp grated ginger
300ml malt vinegar
700g sugar
2 tsp horseradish

Cut the lemons into thick slices, removing the pips and mix with the salt; leave for eight hours.

Put in a food processor and chop until the peel is in small pieces; scrape down well.

Add the remaining ingredients, put in a pan and cook slowly until the mixture goes thick and syrupy.

Store in the fridge in an airtight jar until required.

Serve with skate wings, along with nut brown butter (butter heated in a pan till it starts to burn).

relish

apple & rosemary compôte

serves 4

Peel, core and chop the apples and put them in a pan with the butter. Add the apples and rosemary. Cook till the apple is soft. Push the apples through a sieve adding a little sugar if necessary. Serve warm with seared scallops.

 Good with goat's cheese, grouse and pheasant, duck, turkey or bacon joints. Excellent with hash browns (p32).

2 bramley apples
25g butter
1 sprig rosemary
1 lemon
25g butter
caster sugar
salad leaves
oil for frying

mustard butter

2 tsp white wine vinegar
4 tsp white wine
2 shallots
1 tsp English mustard
4 dsp double cream
250g hard unsalted butter
1 tbsp grain mustard

Chop the shallots very finely and put in a small pan with the vinegar and wine; reduce by two thirds.

Add the English mustard, the cream and reduce a little more.

Add the diced butter and whisk in until amalgamated. Stir in seasonings to taste then pass through a fine sieve.

Great with grilled fish and vegetarian dishes.

As a variation, substitute the grain mustard with chopped herbs such as tarragon, basil, dill or chives.

butters

herb butter

Mix the ingredients together and roll in greaseproof paper or cling film to make a cylinder shape. Chill well before cutting into thick coins. Serve with grills and fish.

1 dsp of mixed chopped herbs (thyme, tarragon, chives, parsley, dill)
125g butter
1 shallot, chopped finely

Marmite butter

Mix the Marmite into the butter till smooth. Shape into rounds and refrigerate to cool.

Put a round of Marmite butter on hot steak, pasta or boiled potatoes before serving, so the butter begins to melt.

dsp Marmite
125g butter

sauces
simple butter sauce

2 shallots
1 tbsp butter
2 tbsp white wine vinegar
5 tbsp white wine
4 dsp whipping cream
250g butter
lemon juice
cayenne pepper

Gently fry finely chopped shallots with a knob of butter for about 20 seconds.

Add the vinegar and wine and reduce to a third. Add the cream and boil for about 30 seconds until quite thick.

Whisk in butter (diced, and cold from the fridge) in four lots, making sure each amount has been whisked in before adding a further quarter of the butter.

Don't allow the sauce to boil at this stage.

Add a drop of lemon juice, a pinch of cayenne pepper and season. If you like a smooth sauce, push through a sieve to remove the shallot.

Keep warm until needed.

Serve with fish, poached eggs or vegetables.

As a variation, added a spoonful of a chopped herb such as coriander, chives or parsley.

Chef's note: using this butter sauce and the Madeira sauce together on the same plate looks very effective and tastes great.

sauces
Madeira sauce

In a pan, add the butter, chopped shallots, bay leaf, thyme and sliced mushrooms and cook until all the water has evaporated and the mushrooms are beginning to stick to the pan (but not burning).

Pour in the Madeira and boil until sticky and only a couple of spoonfuls remain.

Add the chicken stock and repeat as above until there are about eight or nine spoonfuls in the bottom of the pan. Add the veal stock, boil to sauce consistency and about 200ml of liquid are left.

Strain through a sieve to remove the mushrooms, shallots and thyme.

Check for seasoning, but you shouldn't need much sea salt and freshly milled pepper.

Excellent with steak or poultry.

100g button mushrooms
2 shallots
25g unsalted butter
1 bay leaf
200ml Madeira
300ml good chicken stock
300ml beef or veal stock
sprig thyme

fabulously simple Vermouth sauce

2 shallots finely chopped
half bottle Vermouth
1 pint cream

Put the shallots and Vermouth in a pan and boil
gently until the liquid has reduced by half.
Add the cream and gently boil until the
sauce coats the back of the spoon.
Pass through a sieve and keep warm
till needed.

Chef's note: This is a great sauce
for most meats – beef, lamb, pork
and game. Also for meaty white fish
such as turbot, hake or monkfish
(but definitely not tuna).

sauces
mushroom sauce

Gently fry the chopped shallots and sliced mushrooms in a little butter.

Add the white wine and Vermouth and boil rapidly until it has evaporated by two thirds.

Add the cream and bring to the boil and simmer until the sauce is creamy and will coat the back of a spoon.

Season with sea salt and lemon juice, and keep warm until needed.

Chef's note: Great with pan-fried salmon, or chicken, pork steaks or most white fish.

2 shallots
1 glass sweet Vermouth
350ml whipping cream
quarter bottle of fruity or
sweet white wine
300g button mushrooms
2 tsp chopped chervil
lemon juice
butter

honey & vanilla yoghurt

200g sweetened yoghurt
100ml whipping cream
1 leaf gelatine
seeds of 1 vanilla pod
75g honey

Soak the gelatine in cold water. Boil 25ml cream and add the gelatine. Semi whip the remaining cream with honey and vanilla seeds, add the yoghurt and whip again. Fold in the melted gelatine, put in the fridge to set. Good to serve with soft fruits such as bananas, strawberries and raspberries.

strawberry coulis

250g strawberries
80g caster sugar
squeeze of lemon juice

Put all the ingredients in a pan; bring to the boil and simmer for 2-3 minutes. Liquidise; push through a sieve and chill.

simple chocolate sauce

160g chocolate (70% cocoa solids)
200ml whipping cream
80ml water
80g sugar

To make the sauce place all the chocolate and cream in one pan and the water and sugar in another.

Bring both to the boil and whisk together.

Makes a lovely glossy sauce to pour over ice cream or to serve with hot banana soufflé, or fresh strawberries.

116

garnish

Armagnac prunes

Pour the brandy over the prunes and allow to soak for an hour or so.

Put the prunes in a pan with the sugar and bring to the boil.

Dissolve the cornflour with a little water and stir into the hot brandy. Remove from the heat and allow to cool before serving with whipped cream.

12 dried prunes
2 measures of brandy
1 dsp sugar
1 tsp cornflour

Chef's tip: pitted Agen or Elvas prunes are the best. Avoid prunes which are packaged as 'soft and ready to eat' as these are treated with sulphur.

index

garlic

- braised beetroot with sour cream 82
- carrots with tarragon & garlic 78
- favourite cous cous 76
- garlic & parsley pie 26
- goat's cheese & leek risotto 44
- grilled polenta cake 74
- leg of lamb steak, lemon & garlic 66
- spaghetti piedmontese 46
- spinach with garlic 80
- sticky garlic ribs 58

ham

- ham shanks in cider, with cloves 56
- potted ham, tarragon & peppercorns 36

herbs

- best end of lamb in herb crumbs 62
- coriander & chilli dip 107
- herb butter 111
- honey & herb roast pork with crackling 60
- one-hour herb roast chicken 48

hot puddings

- favourite bread & butter pudding 88
- hot banana souffle 98
- spicy chocolate bread & butter pudding 88

mushrooms

- goosnargh chicken, mushrooms & leeks 50
- mushroom sauce 115
- pan-fried salmon & mushroom sauce 40

pork

– honey & herb roast pork with crackling 60
– sticky garlic ribs 58

potato

– black pudding & lancashire cheese hash
  browns with caramelised onions 32
– garlic & parsley pie 26
– gratin dauphinoise 72
– irish stew with onion dumplings 64
– new potato & smoked salmon salad 22
– smoked mackerel & potato pie 26

lamb

– best end of lamb in herb crumbs 62
– irish stew with onion dumplings 64
– leg of lamb steak, lemon & garlic 66

pasta, polenta, rice & cous cous

– favourite cous cous 76
– goat's cheese & leek risotto 44
– grilled polenta cake 74
– spaghetti piedmontese 46

salads

– new potato & smoked salmon salad 22
– seared scallops with salad leaves 24
– torn chicken salad, blue cheese & gems 34

index